N. T. WRIGHT
FOR EVERY...
BIBLE STUDY G...

2 CORINTHIANS

11 STUDIES FOR INDIVIDUALS OR GROUPS

N. T. WRIGHT

WITH PATTY PELL

IVP Connect

An imprint of InterVarsity Press
Downers Grove, Illinois

InterVarsity Press
P.O. Box 1400, Downers Grove, IL 60515-1426
World Wide Web: www.ivpress.com
E-mail: email@ivpress.com

InterVarsity Press® is the book-publishing division of InterVarsity Christian Fellowship/USA®, a
movement of students and faculty active on campus at hundreds of universities, colleges and schools
of nursing in the United States of America, and a member movement of the International Fellowship of
Evangelical Students. For information about local and regional activities, write Public Relations Dept.,
InterVarsity Christian Fellowship/USA, 6400 Schroeder Rd., P.O. Box 7895, Madison, WI 53707-7895, or
visit the IVCF website at <www.intervarsity.org>.

Cover design: Cindy Kiple
Cover image: Paul Knight/Trevillion Images

ISBN 978-0-8308-2188-4

Printed in the United States of America ∞

P	18	17	16	15	14	13	12	11	10	9	8	7	6	5	4	3	2	1
Y	25	24	23	22	21	20	19	18	17	16	15	14	13	12	11	10			

CONTENTS

GETTING THE MOST
OUT OF 2 CORINTHIANS

You watch from a distance as a friend walks down the street. You see him turn and go into a house. He strides in cheerfully and purposefully. You wait for a few minutes. Then you see him come out again—only now you see, to your horror, that he is limping, staggering along, with bruises on his face and blood trickling from one arm. Filled with concern, you also immediately want to know: *what on earth happened in that house?*

The historian, particularly the ancient historian, is often in the position of the puzzled spectator. The historian may have evidence about an early phase of someone's career, and then again a later phase; but what happened in between is often hidden. So it is with Paul. He has gone into the house, striding cheerfully along; we have watched him do so in his first letter to the Corinthians. Now in 2 Corinthians we see him emerge again, battered and bruised. Even his style of writing seems to have changed. But we don't know what happened inside. (For more on this book, also see my *Paul for Everyone: 2 Corinthians*, published by SPCK and Westminster John Knox. This guide is based on that book and was prepared with the help of Patty Pell, for which I am grateful.)

Nor does he tell us what happened. Like many people in the ancient world, he was more interested in what illness or suffering *meant* than in giving us a detailed account of his symptoms. Most of what we know is in the opening of the letter; we can glean a little from things he says later in the letter, but it doesn't amount to much. He simply refers to "the suffering we went through in Asia" (the Roman province of "Asia" was roughly the western half of modern Turkey, with Ephesus in the middle of its west coast where Paul was staying when he wrote 1 Corinthians). Since his conversion (see Acts 9), Paul had been carrying the message of Jesus and the resurrection throughout the Mediterranean region, often with significant opposition and even violence. But what happened in Asia to cause him such distress?

The book of Acts doesn't help much at this point either. The riot that engulfed Paul in Ephesus that is described in Acts 19 may have been part of it. In that passage, things are quieted down by the city officials. But the opposition may have continued in new and nastier ways, leaving Paul feeling, as he says here, that he's received the sentence of death. In fact, his description sounds much like what we would call a nervous breakdown. The load had become too heavy.

The thing he doesn't mention explicitly, but which would be an important factor in his mind and that of his readers, is that illness and suffering in the ancient world were regularly regarded as signs of divine displeasure. Whatever Paul had gone through, it would have been easy for his enemies, or those who were jealous of him, to think to themselves that it probably served him right, that God was most likely punishing him for something or other. Not so, says Paul. These things come not because God is angry but because he wants us to trust him more fully. Paul was breaking new ground. He wanted the Corinthians to understand that this, too, was part of the earth-shattering implication of the gospel.

Paul's theme throughout this letter is the strange royal comfort that comes from the suffering and death, and the new resurrection life, of Israel's Messiah, Jesus, the Lord of the world. This is the letter above all where he explores the meaning of the cross in terms of personal suffering—his own, and that of all the Messiah's people. If in Galatians he is angry, if in Philippians he is joyful, in this letter his deep sorrow, and the raw wounds of his own recent suffering, are very apparent. Yet he is determined to view all of his suffering and all of the troubles of the world through the lens of the gospel.

SUGGESTIONS FOR INDIVIDUAL STUDY

1. As you begin each study, pray that God will speak to you through his Word.

2. Read the introduction to the study and respond to the "Open" question that follows it. This is designed to help you get into the theme of the study.

3. Read and reread the Bible passage to be studied. Each study is designed to help you consider the meaning of the passage in its context. The commentary and questions in this guide are based on my own translation of each passage found in the companion volume to this guide in the For Everyone series on the New Testament (published by SPCK and Westminster John Knox).

4. Write your answers to the questions in the spaces provided or in a personal journal. Each study includes three types of questions: observation questions, which ask about the basic facts in the passage; interpretation questions, which delve into the meaning of the passage; and application questions, which help you discover the implications of the text for growing in Christ. Writing out your responses can bring clarity and deeper understanding of yourself and of God's Word.

5. Each session features selected comments from the For Everyone series. These notes provide further biblical and cultural background and contextual information. They are designed not to answer the questions for you but to help you along as you study the Bible for yourself. For even more reflections on each passage, you may wish to have on hand a copy of the companion volume from the For Everyone series as you work through this study guide.

6. Use the guidelines in the "Pray" section to focus on God, thanking him for what you have learned and praying about the applications that have come to mind.

SUGGESTIONS FOR GROUP MEMBERS

1. Come to the study prepared. Follow the suggestions for individual

study mentioned above. You will find that careful preparation will greatly enrich your time spent in group discussion.

2. Be willing to participate in the discussion. The leader of your group will not be lecturing. Instead, she or he will be asking the questions found in this guide and encouraging the members of the group to discuss what they have learned.

3. Stick to the topic being discussed. These studies focus on a particular passage of Scripture. Only rarely should you refer to other portions of the Bible or outside sources. This allows for everyone to participate on equal ground and for in-depth study.

4. Be sensitive to the other members of the group. Listen attentively when they describe what they have learned. You may be surprised by their insights! Each question assumes a variety of answers. Many questions do not have "right" answers, particularly questions that aim at meaning or application. Instead the questions push us to explore the passage more thoroughly.

   When possible, link what you say to the comments of others. Also, be affirming whenever you can. This will encourage some of the more hesitant members of the group to participate.

5. Be careful not to dominate the discussion. We are sometimes so eager to express our thoughts that we leave too little opportunity for others to respond. By all means participate! But allow others to also.

6. Expect God to teach you through the passage being discussed and through the other members of the group. Pray that you will have an enjoyable and profitable time together, but also that as a result of the study you will find ways that you can take action individually and/ or as a group.

7. It will be helpful for groups to follow a few basic guidelines. These guidelines, which you may wish to adapt to your situation, should be read at the beginning of the first session.

   • Anything said in the group is considered confidential and will not be discussed outside the group unless specific permission is given to do so.

- We will provide time for each person present to talk if he or she feels comfortable doing so.

- We will talk about ourselves and our own situations, avoiding conversation about other people.

- We will listen attentively to each other.

- We will be very cautious about giving advice.

Additional suggestions for the group leader can be found at the back of the guide.

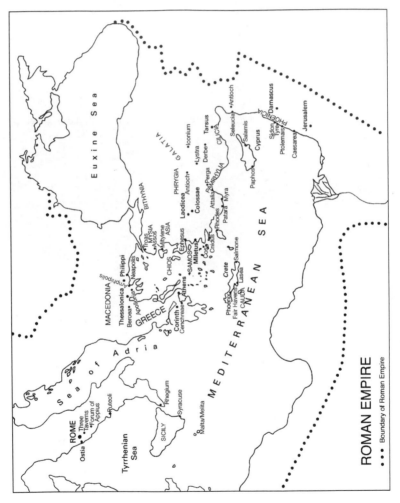

The Eastern Mediterranean in the First Century A.D.

ROMAN EMPIRE
••••• Boundary of Roman Empire

1

THE GOD OF ALL COMFORT

2 Corinthians 1:1–2:4

The gospel, as Paul summarizes it in 1 Corinthians 15:3-8, is about Jesus the Messiah: that he died for our sins according to the Scriptures, that he was buried, and that he was raised on the third day according to the Scriptures. It matters vitally to Paul that these were real events which really took place. But it matters just as much that they become the lens through which the whole world can be seen in proper focus, the grid on which all reality and experience can be plotted. And here, turning his thoughts into prayer, we see what that might mean.

OPEN

Describe a time when you needed comfort.

STUDY

1. *Read 2 Corinthians 1:1-14.* Paul often begins the main part of his letters with a prayer in which he lays before God the main theme he wants to get across to his readers. There is no problem discovering

what that is in this case. *Comfort* is mentioned multiple times in just five verses. How is *comfort* different from other words that Paul could have used such as *console?*

2. What is the pattern of interchange that Paul describes between the Messiah and his followers in 1:1-7 and between the apostle and the church?

3. How have you seen this dynamic at work yourself?

4. What does Paul say he has been feeling or experiencing in 1:8-14?

5. What does he say is the purpose for his suffering?

6. Paul has reached a point where the night has become totally dark and all hope of dawn has disappeared. His burden is heavy and his natural resources of energy are worn down to nothing. What else is Paul hoping for in describing all of this to the Corinthians in 1:8-14?

7. Who can you be connected to in prayer as Paul describes?

8. *Read 2 Corinthians 1:15–2:4.* The Corinthians had apparently been upset to get messages saying first one thing about Paul's visits and then another. To get from Ephesus to Corinth by sea was a journey of two hundred and fifty miles, a trip traders made all the time. Paul himself had done it before. He seemed to be switching to and fro, however. Even though Paul had good reasons for his change of plans, the Corinthians got the impression that he was vacillating.

   Since Paul doesn't go into detail, we can only make informed guesses about the specific circumstances referred to in 1:23–2:4. What do you think is causing his apparent indecisiveness?

9. What were Paul's intentions?

10. In the middle of his explanation about his changes of plans, what aspects of God in Christ does Paul emphasize are always certain, ways that the gospel says "yes" (1:18-22)?

   Amen is one of the few Hebrew words spoken around the world to-day, though most people don't realize where it comes from. When someone says a prayer, and other people want to associate themselves with it, they say *amen*, which means "Yes!" or "I agree!" or "That's what I want to say too!"

11. Why is coming back to the bedrock of our faith in these ways important in the uncertainties of life?

12. Paul's words in this first chapter of 2 Corinthians depict the deep suffering he has been experiencing in his ministry and how the gospel message itself gives him hope to continue. What aspects of this chapter speak to you and give you hope as you think about your own areas of suffering?

PRAY

Pray for those places in life where there is suffering and sadness. Specifically use the words of Paul in this chapter in your prayers of encouragement and comfort.

NOTE ON 2 CORINTHIANS 1:23–2:4

We can't know for sure what was behind Paul's change of plans. Paul apparently made a brief visit to Corinth to follow up on the problems he had written about in 1 Corinthians. It seems the visit didn't go well, that there were opposition and complaints about him (as 2 Corinthians suggests later on). Paul returned to Ephesus, we assume, in deep distress and wrote another letter which wasn't preserved (2:3-4). This seemed to have only made matters worse. So he decided not to come again to spare them more distress (1:23) or at least to delay until he could prepare the groundwork for his visit through correspondence.

THE LETTER AND THE SPIRIT

2 Corinthians 2:5–3:18

The sense of smell was highly valued in the ancient world. The very mention of "sweet-smelling knowledge" in this passage of 2 Corinthians could have awakened many different associations in the minds of ancient readers. Paul may well have more than one scent in mind.

They might have thought of sacrifice in a temple, perhaps in the temple in Jerusalem. People believed that the divinity would smell the sweet smell of the sacrifice and be pleased. Or they might have simply thought of incense, which was regularly used to indicate the presence of the divinity, in both pagan and Jewish worship.

OPEN

What smell brings back the most vibrant and clear memories for you?

STUDY

1. *Read 2 Corinthians 2:5-17.* We do not know all the specifics of the circumstance that seems to be referred to in 2:5-11. The person in

question may perhaps be the same person Paul denounced in 1 Corinthians 5:1-5, the man who had been living with his father's wife. He had then instructed that the man should be dismissed from the Christian fellowship. But what we do know is that in response to one of Paul's appeals, the church did indeed put someone under extremely severe discipline.

How does Paul want the Corinthian church to behave toward this member who has been put under severe discipline?

2. How does 2:5-11 illustrate the extent to which the community's life is bound up together?

3. Why are both a willingness to deal with sin and a willingness to forgive necessary in the right sequence and in the right balance?

4. When a king or general had won a notable military victory, the whole city would turn out to welcome him and his troops as they came home in jubilation. They would bring with them the prisoners they had taken (who would later be killed publicly); they would display the booty they had plundered; and they would do everything to make it clear to their own people that they had indeed been victorious.

What is Paul communicating in 2:12-17 with the image of a triumphal military procession?

5. How do we rise to the challenge Paul is talking about in 2:14-16?

6. *Read 2 Corinthians 3.* Paul continues with the discussion about his role as an apostle in 3:1-6. What seems to be the problem that Paul is responding to?

7. What does he mean when he refers to the Corinthians themselves as his letter of recommendation?

8. In 3:3 Paul alludes to Jeremiah 31:33 where the prophet spoke of a new covenant, superseding the covenant with Moses, in which God puts the law into people's hearts.

   What are practical ways we can be stewards or ministers of the new covenant, not of the letter that kills but of the Spirit that gives life (3:6)?

9. Paul uses the story from Exodus 34:29-35 where Moses finds himself pleading for the Israelites after they worship a golden calf. This deep and heartfelt prayer called forth from God a fresh revelation of himself and Moses glimpsed God's glory so much that he had to cover his shining face with a veil because the Israelites were afraid

of him. Only when Moses turned back to the Lord in the tabernacle did he remove the veil.

What argument is Paul making by using this story in 3:7-11?

10. How does Paul continue to use the Exodus 34 passage to explain in 3:12-18 why he is so bold in his ministry?

11. Paul says in 3:18 that when he and the Corinthians look at each other with unveiled faces, they actually see the glory of the Lord reflected in each other. They see each other being transformed from one degree of glory to another by the Spirit. Why would this be so astonishing?

12. What practical differences would it make in your Christian community if you began seeing each other this way?

PRAY

Reflect on and thank God for the amazing way the Spirit has made a new covenant in the hearts of Christians around you and transformed them so that they reflect God's glory.

NOTE ON 2 CORINTHIANS 2:12-13

Paul describes his anxious journey north from Ephesus to Troas (ancient Troy, near the coast), and then across to Macedonia. He was anxious because he had sent Titus ahead of him to Corinth to find out the current mood and tell him what sort of reception he might expect. He had thought that Titus would be coming back and would meet him at Troas, but he wasn't there. We have to wait until 2 Corinthians 7:5 to pick up the thread of this travel story again, with Titus finally meeting Paul and bringing good news.

3

Treasure in
Earthenware Pots

2 Corinthians 4

Sir Oliver Franks held a demanding job shortly after the Second
World War, at the time when the Cold War began and the North Atlantic Treaty Organization was set up. He was British Ambassador to the
United States. As ambassador, he was in touch, often on a daily basis,
with the president on one side of the Atlantic and the prime minister on
the other.

Franks frequently needed to get urgent and top-secret messages
between Washington and London. It was far too risky to make tele-
phone calls, but there was a diplomatic bag which went to and fro
each day, bringing confidential documents by air across the Atlantic.
That was the method he used for most of his important and confidential messages. But when something was utterly top-secret and desperately urgent, he wouldn't trust it to a bag which everybody knew
was important. He would put it into an ordinary envelope and send it
through the regular mail.

What Paul is saying in 2 Corinthians 4 is that there is no chance of
anyone confusing the content of the envelope with the very ordinary,
unremarkable envelope itself. The messenger is not important; what

matters, vitally and urgently, is the message. The Corinthians have been looking at the envelope—at Paul's own public figure, his speaking style, at his suffering—and have concluded that there is nothing at all remarkable about him. He ought to look more important than that, surely, if he really is a messenger with a message from God.

Paul says that they are missing the point!

OPEN

When have you seen someone try to explain something and the people to whom it was being explained just were not getting the point?

STUDY

1. *Read 2 Corinthians 4.* Paul is still responding to accusations here about the way he conducts his ministry. From what he says in 4:1-6, what allegations was he facing?

2. What does Paul communicate with the image of light in verses 4-6?

3. According to 4:1-6, what does Paul see as his job description?

4. Paul begins a description in verses 7-12 that will continue on and off throughout the rest of the letter of what life is like for a genuine apostle. How does Paul view his recent experiences?

5. What is Paul trying to communicate by using the image of earthenware pots?

6. How is it that both life and death can be at work in Paul at the same time?

7. In the present passage, Paul says he is persecuted but not abandoned; cast down but not destroyed. What he says here he says with the benefit of hindsight, but he has not forgotten that it did not feel like that when it was going on. When we read chapter 1 we discovered that *at the time* it really felt as though he *was* being crushed, abandoned and destroyed. How is this an encouragement for us when we go through persecution, temptation, suffering, bereavement, tragedy or sorrow?

8. Think of a time when you felt crushed and abandoned, but now as you look back, you realize that you were not overcome. How were you actually living out the nature of the gospel in that situation?

9. Paul sometimes quotes a short line from the Bible when he wants his readers to recall a whole story or the whole setting and mood of a passage. In verse 13, he quotes Psalm 116:10. Look over Psalm 116. How does this psalm fit together with 4:13-18?

10. It is easy to assume that Paul, in 4:16-18, is saying that bodily things, outward things, don't matter. It's easy to imagine that he is insisting on true reality being non-bodily things, "spiritual" things in that sense. But, as his other writings (and indeed the next chapter) make clear, this is not the case.

    What two worlds are instead being contrasted in these verses?

11. Looking back over all of chapter 4, why is Paul not losing heart, even though his suffering might make it look as if he would?

12. Paul has laid out a complete picture of the future resurrection and how it relates to present suffering. How do the future resurrection and the words of this chapter help you face the present suffering in your own life that threatens to overwhelm you and rob you of your hope and heart?

PRAY

Rewrite verses 8-9 using your own words to describe how you feel. Use these rewritten verses to pray for the Lord's strength and hope.

4

NEW CREATION, NEW MINISTRY

2 Corinthians 5:1–6:2

Oₙe of the sights that can be visited in the ancient city of Corinth is the judgment seat. In the city was the Forum, which was lined with shops, temples and public buildings. The most important public buildings were the government headquarters; and there, in the middle, is the place where, in Paul's day, the Roman governor would sit to dispense justice, to try cases. The judgment seat. That is, of course, where Paul himself ended up on his first visit, according to Acts 18:12-17.

In many modern societies, justice is dispensed behind closed doors. Most people don't see the inside of a courtroom for themselves more than once or twice in their lives. In most ancient towns it wasn't like that. Justice was very public, and everybody could see what was going on.

The picture Paul draws in chapter 5 is that of everybody appearing before the judgment seat of the Messiah. This is one of the clearest statements of the last judgment in Paul's writings, and indeed anywhere in the New Testament.

OPEN

What images come to mind when you think of the last judgment?

STUDY

1. *Read 2 Corinthians 5:1–10.* What is Paul longing for in verses 1-5?

2. How does Paul use the images of a house and clothing in 5:1-5 to describe our future existence?

3. In what ways are you or those you know burdened by your present physical existence?

4. The Christian hope for the future is not about becoming *disembodied* but about being *reembodied*. We don't, as Paul says, want to turn out to be "naked," a bare spirit or soul without any "clothing." In fact, the hope he expresses in 5:4 is seen in terms of putting more clothes on top of the ones we're wearing already. We don't want to be *unclothed*, but to be *more fully clothed*. The transformation he has in mind, exactly as in 1 Corinthians 15, is that whereas the present body is doomed to die, heading for corruption and decay, our resurrection body to come will be full of a life that nothing can harm or destroy. The Spirit who raised Jesus bodily from the dead to a new kind of transphysical life is, as Paul says in verse 5, the same Spirit we have now who acts as our down payment for our new embodied, decay-free existence-to-come.

    How does this further explain what Paul meant in 3:10-12 that though he carries death about with him, he also carries life?

5. Paul's picture of the resurrection of the body in 5:1-5 is not a picture of something that happens immediately after death, but of something that happens to enable us to stand before the Lord when he comes as judge. How does Paul describe our situation between the time of our death and the time of the final judgment in 5:6-10?

6. What does living by faith look like as opposed to living by sight or living by doubt (5:7)?

7. Elsewhere Paul speaks of justification by faith, but here he speaks of doing our best to please the Lord because one day we will stand before him to receive the reward or recompense for what we have done. Paul sees no conflict between justification by faith and rewards to come. When he says that "there is no condemnation for those in the Messiah" (Romans 8:1), he at once explains that this is because (a) God has condemned sin in the Messiah, so ultimate condemnation is impossible for those who are "in him," and (b) God has given his Spirit to the Messiah's people, and the Spirit will enable them to become, in their moral behavior, the people he has already declared them to be in justification.

How does 5:7-9 affirm the importance of both faith and behavior?

8. *Read 2 Corinthians 5:11–6:2.* According to 5:11-15, why does Paul behave the way he does, in ways that are so different from what the Corinthians expect?

9. In 2 Corinthians 5:16 Paul speaks of a "worldly point of view" (NIV) or "according to the flesh" (ESV) or as I translate it: "a merely human point of view." Here Paul is contrasting, on the one hand, the old human world that is decaying and will pass away with, on the other hand, the new world to come made possible by Jesus' death and resurrection. The same is true of the Messiah himself. Jesus' aim was not to establish a purely human, worldly, fleshly kingdom that would decay. Instead he is creating an entirely new world.

What does Paul go on to say has been changed because of the Messiah (5:16–6:2)?

10. What does it look like to be a "new creation" (5:17)?

11. How is this final section (5:16–6:2) a further discussion of Paul's ministry and job description?

12. In what ways can you live out your calling as a believer to be a "minister of reconciliation" like Paul?

PRAY

Spend time thanking God for all the things in your life that have been made new. Then, pray for friends and family who are not yet reconciled to God.

NOTE ON 2 CORINTHIANS 5:1-5

When Paul says our new body is not made with human hands (5:1), he is using a regular Jewish phrase which contrasts something given or done by God himself with something that mere humans have produced. The resurrection body, then, will be similar to the present one in some respects and quite different in others. It's hard to imagine just what it will be like; the resurrection of Jesus himself was regarded by Paul and others in the early church as the model and prototype of the one that is to come, but that doesn't tell us much except that it really is what we would call a body but with startling new properties.

The idea of "going to heaven" as a final destination can trick people into imagining that the Christian teaching about what happens after death is that you leave the body behind and go off into a non-bodily state where the "soul" is either saved or lost. That is clearly wrong. Paul argues that we shall be given new bodies, not immediately after we die (unless the Lord returns then), but on the great day of resurrection which lies in the future.

5

GOD'S SERVANTS AT WORK

2 Corinthians 6:3–7:1

The Corinthians have been grumpy with Paul, refusing to acknowledge that his style of ministry is the genuine thing. They have wanted someone different—perhaps an actual person who is even now in Corinth, gathering support. And they have criticized Paul for not being the right sort, not doing the right things.

Because of this, in chapter 6, Paul opens his heart in a long burst of rhetoric. This is the sort of person I have been, he says. Why don't I tell you exactly how it's been for me! Paul presses on, trying everything to break through the crust of indifference and make them see: this is what it means to follow a crucified Messiah! This is what it means to be an apostle of the world's true Lord!

OPEN

When have you felt misunderstood? Describe the situation.

STUDY

1. *Read 2 Corinthians 6:3-13.* In 6:4-10, Paul gives a splendid catalog of what he's had to do and face over his years of relentless travel and proclamation. What are the different kinds of things Paul mentions?

2. How did Paul respond to his hardships?

3. What does Paul want the Corinthians to understand about him and his ministry through this list?

4. Think of the leaders in your Christian community and the kinds of criticisms they may have faced. How do Paul's comments help us see things from their perspective?

5. The extraordinary balance of this list reveals the mark of genuine Christian authenticity. Christians sometimes talk as if life were simply a matter of glory, of celebration, of the Lord providing all our needs and everything going forward without a hitch.

   What are the dangers of living in this kind of shallowness instead of living in the truth of life as Paul depicts in this passage?

6. In what ways does being honest about the struggles and trials, as well as the joys and celebrations, of the Christian life help you open your heart to others?

7. What kind of an invitation is Paul making to the Corinthians in 6:11-13?

8. What is Paul's emotion behind the invitation he makes?

9. *Read 2 Corinthians 6:14–7:1.* What contrasts does Paul use in 6:14–7:1 to explain why partnerships with unbelievers should be avoided?

The basic command in 6:14 could refer to any sort of partnership, such as in business. But its most obvious reference is to marriage. In 1 Corinthians 7:12-16 Paul addresses the question of people who become Christians when their spouse does not, and tells them not to separate unless the unbelieving spouse wants to. But in verse 39 of that same chapter he makes it clear that when contracting a fresh marriage it is important that this be only "in the Lord," in other words, to a fellow Christian.

10. In 6:16-18 Paul is quoting from several Old Testament texts. What do they emphasize about God and God's people?

11. How, therefore, should the Corinthians (and how should we) view the world and live in it?

PRAY

Be open with God about the difficulties and the joys you and others face in your relationship with the Lord. Pray for your Christian leaders who no doubt are receiving various kinds of criticisms and complaints.

6

OUR BOASTING
PROVED TRUE!

2 Corinthians 7:2-16

If you want to know what it looks like and feels like to commit it all to God, come with Paul as he struggles along the road, exhausted and emotionally drained after his terrible experiences in Ephesus. He goes north to Troas, then across the waterway and on through Macedonia. With every step of the way he was praying and hoping, but it was a constant tussle against fears that welled up inside and opposition that attacked him all around. Every day when he didn't find Titus waiting for him was another disappointment; every day he went on, hoping for good news but bracing for the worst.

The journey through Macedonia, to the point where Titus, coming north from Corinth, finally met up with Paul, may explain the rather jerky sequence of paragraphs at this point in the letter. It may well be that Paul dictated the letter in bits as he was on the road, stopping night after night in different places. We can never be sure, but what we can be sure of is that Paul is writing eagerly back to the Corinthians after Titus has brought news from them.

OPEN

What is your image of what a successful Christian ought to look like?

STUDY

1. *Read 2 Corinthians 7:2-16.* What was the emotional and physical state of Paul described throughout verses 2-10?

2. What is Paul's main concern or desire for the Corinthians in verses 2-10?

3. The tables have, it seems, been turned. Paul was anxious that the Corinthians were cross with him, ready to rebel against his authority, and now Titus has made it clear that *they* are anxious about what state of mind *he* will be in when he arrives (vv. 6-7). All of this leads Paul to some profound reflections on sadness.

   How does Paul affirm both his love for the Corinthians and the sorrow he may have caused them?

4. How have you seen sadness and repentance go together?

5. What is the difference between God's way of sadness and the world's way of sadness?

6. How does 7:2-10 compare with your vision of the "successful" or "normal" Christian life?

7. In 2 Corinthians 2:5-8 Paul refers to the person the church had to discipline. In 7:11-13 he mentions the situation again and wants to reassure them that they have acted properly in this matter.

   What does Paul say is providing him some comfort (7:2-16)?

8. If you write a letter to someone very dear to you, surely you are more likely to tell them how fond *you* are of *them*, not how fond they are of you. Why does Paul in verse 12 need to tell the Corinthians how keen *they* are on *him*?

9. How is the truthfulness of Paul's boast to Titus another sign that God is backing up Paul's general truthfulness and character?

10. We see that it will take both humble repentance and deep expressions of fondness to resolve the trouble and tension in Paul's relationship with the Corinthians. Why are both of these necessary for true reconciliation?

11. What does Paul praise the Corinthians for in these verses?

12. What boasts could you confidently make to others about your church or a fellow believer?

PRAY

Pray silently and ask God to help you approach difficult relationships with humility and repentance. Then, spend a few minutes praying for those with whom you are having conflict. Seek God's love and grace for these persons.

GOD LOVES A
CHEERFUL GIVER

2 Corinthians 8:1–9:15

In chapters 8 and 9 Paul is walking on eggshells, yet he somehow gets away with it. His overall purpose is to make sure that by the time he arrives in Corinth the church will have put aside the full amount of money they are going to contribute for the impoverished Jerusalem church. Despite the agony in the relationship between him and the church in the intervening period he is now determined to press ahead and complete the task.

He wants them to share in the great project he has in hand: demonstrating to the Gentile churches that they are part of the same family as the Jewish Christians in Jerusalem, and demonstrating to the Jerusalem Christians that the strange, uncircumcised Gentiles are fellow members with them in God's renewed people. He is desperately concerned for the unity of the whole Christian family, and he has glimpsed, as part of his missionary vocation, the possibility of doing something so striking, so remarkable, so practical that it will establish a benchmark for generations to come.

OPEN

How do you react when you begin to hear someone preach about financial giving?

STUDY

1. *Read 2 Corinthians 8:1-24.* The sense that Paul has a delicate task in 2 Corinthians 8–9 is suggested in that he never once in these two chapters uses any of the Greek words for "money" itself. Instead he phrases everything very indirectly.

    What factors make his project of persuading Gentile churches to hand over money to Jerusalem so tricky that he would need to be this indirect?

2. Macedonia is the area that roughly corresponds today with northern Greece (see map on p. 10). Describe the character of the Macedonian churches.

3. How do you think people and churches become this way?

4. How is Paul using the word *grace* in 8:1-7?

5. In 8:8-15 what is Paul urging the Corinthians to do?

6. At the center of Paul's appeal in 8:9 is the death and resurrection of Jesus. How does this truth about Jesus become a practical, down-to-earth way of life for his people?

Paul quotes from Exodus 16:18 in 2 Corinthians 8:15. In this way he reminds the Corinthians not just of the particular incident of the manna in the wilderness (Exodus 16:1-18) but of the whole Exodus story. He reminds them how God renews and redeems his people as they travel through the present life and world toward their promised inheritance. Paul is grounding his urgent appeal for generous giving both on the grace of the Lord Jesus and on the underlying purpose of God, which is to ensure that his people do not go hungry on their journey home.

7. Paul writes about sending two "brothers" with Titus (8:18, 22). It is frustrating that Paul doesn't name these other "brothers." We would like to know who they were; we'd also like to know why Paul has decided to refer to them in this oblique, anonymous fashion. Perhaps he is anxious that if the letter falls into the wrong hands these men might then be the targets of unwelcome attention as being possible carriers of large sums of money.

In any case, in 8:16-24 why does Paul find it important to send several others with Titus?

8. What kinds of precautions and procedures are important to put in place in Christian groups today where fundraising and finances are concerned so that everything looks right to God and others?

9. *Read 2 Corinthians 9:1-15.* Paul gives the impression that he cared deeply about every stage of his own planning, and thought hard about all the people involved and how they would be affected. In 9:1-5 what are the key things he wants to make sure are the case in the process of collecting the gift?

10. Attempting to tell people to do something they don't particularly want to do is difficult. If you are a forceful enough character, people may eventually do what you want; but they won't enjoy it, and you may damage some relationships on the way. It is far better to turn their minds around so that they see everything—God, the world, the church, themselves—in a different light, and then the behavior will come naturally.

    How is Paul attempting to turn the minds of the Corinthians around in 9:6-15 and give them a new, bigger way of seeing things?

11. How can this be motivation for generous and cheerful giving?

12. What holds you back from giving generously to God's people and God's work?

13. Where do you feel God might be calling you to be a generous and cheerful giver?

PRAY

Engage in a time of listening prayer. Ask God to show you what obstacles may be in your heart which keep you from generous and cheerful giving. Pray for his power to release you from those obstacles.

8

BOASTING IN THE LORD

2 Corinthians 10

Paul now turns back to the theme which dominated the early part of his letter—his standing with the Corinthians, and the attacks that some in the church have made against his style, his ministry, his very apostleship. He does this by speaking about the weapons used in battle. Weapons are what you need for the battle against all ideas, arguments, philosophies and worldviews that set themselves up against the knowledge of the true God.

Paul knew what he was talking about: the world of ancient Greece, Turkey, Syria and Palestine was teeming with religions and cults, philosophies and teachings, dark magic and high-flown wisdom, arcane rituals and passionately held ideals. But there was only one place where the power of the true God, the Creator of the world, had been fully and finally unveiled, and that was in the death and resurrection of Jesus, the Messiah. Paul was determined to confront the human-made systems of thought which, though usually containing some glimmers of truth, actually led people away from knowledge of the true God rather than toward him.

OPEN

What are the ideas, arguments, philosophies, movements and religious teachings that have wide influence in the world today? What makes them appealing?

STUDY

1. *Read 2 Corinthians 10.* What is Paul's strategy in the battle for the mind described in verses 1-6?

2. At the heart of Paul's strategy is verse 5. What does it look like in daily life to take every thought prisoner?

3. Which of the ideas, philosophies and religious teachings mentioned at the beginning of this study trouble you or cause doubt? Explain.

4. What steps can you take to deal with these questions constructively?

5. The battle for the mind has to be fought not only outside the church but inside it as well. Paul is beginning once more to do this in verses 1-11. He now knows that the church as a whole is well disposed toward him, but there are still some who might be inclined to rebel.

What questions or challenges are some members of the church still confronting Paul with?

6. How do verses 7-11 fit with verses 1-6 in showing Paul's response to these challenges?

7. Many people today find Paul's boldness worrying. They don't like thinking of a Christian teacher being so confrontational. But we can't have it both ways. Paul has been accused of being weak and insignificant. He boldly shows how they are mistaken.

How can boldness and humility appropriately be combined in our relationships and ministry?

8. We meet the same problem in 10:12 as earlier: the question of people who "commend" or recommend themselves. How do Paul's standards of measurement differ from those of the people recommending themselves?

9. What does Paul say is the standard and the commission that he received from God by which he is to be measured?

10. What it all comes down to is the true nature of the Christian "boast": anyone who boasts should boast in the Lord! Paul has already quoted Jeremiah 9:23-24 in the first letter to Corinth and now he quotes it again. What does it look like to "boast in the Lord"?

11. For what specific things can you "boast in the Lord" right now?

12. How does the practice of boasting in the Lord help in the battle for the mind?

PRAY

Thank God for the ways you can boast in him. Ask the Holy Spirit to help you discern which thoughts and ideas are getting in the way of people coming to know the true God, and to enable you to capture them so that they can serve Christ instead.

9

BOASTING OF WEAKNESSES

2 Corinthians 11

Many movies and novels in the Western world have as a stock theme the marriage ceremony that goes wrong at the last minute. It may be the man who rushes into the service moments before his true love marries another or the bride who simply keeps running away from the ceremony at the last moment.

In Paul's world, especially his Jewish world, most marriages would be arranged by the parents, often when the bride at least was, by Western standards, very young. Everything has been agreed; the husband-to-be is delighted, and so is the bride—or at least she was; but the father is suddenly worried that she is going to get cold feet. Paul uses this sort of wedding scenario to begin chapter 11 and to continue his response and explanation to the "teachers" causing problems in Corinth.

OPEN

What's one of your favorite stories of things gone wrong at weddings—whether from books or movies, or weddings you've attended or heard about?

STUDY

1. *Read 2 Corinthians 11:1-15.* How does Paul use the wedding image and the temptation and rebellion image from Genesis in verses 1-6 to show his concern for the Corinthian church?

2. It looks as though in 11:1-6 Paul is now accusing the teachers (who came to Corinth after he left) of something besides questioning his credentials or qualifications. What concerns Paul?

3. What does the single-minded devotion to Christ mentioned in verse 3 look like in practice?

4. Why, according to Paul in 11:7-15, was it so important for him to avoid being a financial burden to the Corinthian church?

5. In what ways was this strategy of Paul's turned against him?

6. The teachers in Corinth had been *accusing* Paul of all kinds of things of which he knew he was not guilty. In traditional biblical and Jewish thinking, the "satan" was the accuser, the director of public prosecutions for the heavenly court. (The Hebrew word we transliterate as *satan* means "accuser.") It was his job to accuse people, to bring charges against all wrongdoers. In order to have charges to bring, the satan seems to have taken to whispering ideas into people's ears . . . and so has become the tempter as well as the prosecutor.

Why does Paul find these accusations so troubling?

7. *Read 2 Corinthians 11:16-33.* How is Paul playing the fool and teasing the Corinthians, but at the same time making his own point in verses 16-21?

8. Throughout his two letters to Corinth, Paul has been aware that the young church is in danger of being sucked into the ordinary cultural life of their city and district. The teachers have been moving in that direction by recommending themselves and wallowing in a culture of fame, success and showy rhetoric.

What Paul lists in verses 21-33 are not the sort of accomplishments and honors one would expect from someone trying to boast. Why does Paul catalog these experiences?

9. In ancient Rome the *corona muralis,* the "crown of the wall," was the highest military honor the empire gave, awarded to a soldier who, in the siege of a city, was the first one over the wall. This was a brave and courageous (and perhaps crazy) accomplishment since the enemy would be shooting arrows down at those climbing up the ladder, perhaps pouring boiling liquids on top of them and pushing the ladders over backward. After surviving the ordeal, to claim the award a soldier would need to return to Rome and swear a solemn oath, invoking the gods to witness that he was telling the truth that he was the first one over the wall.

   How, in 11:31-33, is Paul carefully following this example but also turning it upside down?

10. Somehow the church in Corinth, and the church today, has to learn to stand normal cultural values on their head, to live the upside-down life (which would actually be the right-way-up life) of the true servants of the Messiah.

   In what particular ways could we, individually or as a Christian community, turn the world's values upside down?

11. What weaknesses can we boast in? How might we do this?

PRAY

Spend time praising God for his upside-down gospel and that he uses our weaknesses for his purposes. Confess the tendency to boast in the things that the world admires.

NOTE ON 2 CORINTHIANS 11:4

Paul accuses some of preaching another gospel in Galatians 1:6-9. But these are likely not the same teachers nor the same incorrect teaching. It is more likely that Paul has in mind the same teachers as he had mentioned earlier in 2 Corinthians. Now he's simply homing in on his real criticism. It isn't that they are actually talking about a completely different person than the first-century Jewish man who was a teacher from Nazareth and was crucified under Pontius Pilate. It isn't that they claim to be offering an entirely different Spirit from the one the Corinthians received. It isn't that they are announcing a gospel which has nothing in common with the one Paul summarizes in 1 Corinthians 15:3-8. No, the problem is more subtle.

The true gospel is the message of the crucified Lord. And the teachers who have come to Corinth after Paul left have been quietly toning down the hard, rough edge of the gospel. It doesn't fit with their social and cultural aspirations. It doesn't sound so good in terms of rhetorical style. In particular, it doesn't give them the reputation and status they were hoping for. If you really believe in the suffering Messiah, and pattern your life accordingly, they think, you might end up looking like . . . yes. Like Paul. And that's what they don't want.

The Signs of
a True Apostle

2 Corinthians 12:1-18

Daedalus was a legendary Greek sculptor and craftsman, famous for his clever inventions. He had gone to Crete, where he worked for the equally famous king, Minos, and built for him the great labyrinth, which comes into other ancient stories. When Daedalus wanted to leave the island again, the king would not let him, so he applied his inventor's brain to the problem and figured out a way to fly. He made wings out of birds' feathers and attached them to his arms and shoulders with wax. He did the same for his son, Icarus.

Off they flew, and were heading back to mainland Greece; but Icarus became too excited by this new form of travel and wanted to fly, not onwards to their destination, but upwards toward the sun. Daedalus did his best to warn him of the danger, but the headstrong Icarus didn't listen. As he got closer to the sun, the heat began to melt the wax holding his wings. Off came the feathers, and Icarus fell into the sea and drowned.

The moral lesson of the story is known in many cultures. Don't fly too high or you may come to a bad end. Don't be too proud or everything may go horribly wrong. What we find in this chapter of 2 Corinthians is the more particularly Christian version of this same point.

OPEN

Describe someone in the news whose pride or arrogance caused big problems.

STUDY

1. *Read 2 Corinthians 12:1-18.* Paul began teasing the Corinthians by "boasting" in his own experiences in chapter 11. He continues this list in this chapter in verses 1-5. Paul refuses to brag in the way the other teachers in Corinth probably were about their spiritual experiences. Instead he talks about "someone" this happened to (even though it becomes clear by verse 7 that he is indeed talking about himself).

   Why would Paul have chosen to list these experiences as a part of his boasting?

2. Paul moves from boasting to describing the "thorn" in the flesh that was given to him in verses 6-10. There has been endless speculation about what this was. A recurrent disease is the most likely guess, but we have no idea what sort. Or it might simply be the regular persecution which Paul always suffered. We just don't know for sure.

   What does Paul say was the purpose of the thorn in his life?

3. When have you seen God's "no" to a prayer bring about growth in character, like Paul's "thorn" did?

When speaking of the extraordinary spiritual experience of going to paradise, Paul then, likely in contrast to the other Corinthian teachers, had nothing specific to teach about what he'd heard or seen. Ironically, Paul at last reveals a direct word that he has received from God in verse 9, but it isn't a word that will let him or anyone else become puffed up in their own self-importance.

4. How is verse 9 consistent with the things Paul has been writing about in chapters 10 and 11?

5. What does it look like to live out the truth of this verse in everyday ways?

6. As Paul says in 12:11, he has been forced into boasting in this letter, though he has made sure he has boasted of all the wrong things. Yet he does offer a "letter of recommendation." This has been a running theme from early in the letter (3:1; 4:2; 5:12; 6:4; 10:12, 18). Indeed, it seems to have been one of the main reasons Paul was writing at all.

   What sort of recommendation does he ultimately say he really ought to offer?

7. In what ways does Paul say in verses 11-18 that he is not inferior to the "super-apostles"?

8. What does Paul communicate in verses 11-18 when he uses the image of a family?

9. The issue of money comes up again in 12:11-18. What implied accusations does he once again respond to and with what answers?

10. Paul faced a number of challenges and accusations from the teachers in Corinth. True gospel ministry, truly apostolic work, is powerful and effective—but will almost certainly be misunderstood and attacked, including by those who ought to know better. We must not ignore the armory of tricks that the satan has at his disposal.

As we look back over this chapter and the entire letter, what do we learn from Paul's example about proper ways of handling such attacks?

PRAY

Intercede for others in situations where there is attack, misunderstanding and pain in the tasks of ministry.

11

Test Yourselves!

2 Corinthians 12:19–13:13

Three of the letters in the New Testament—the two letters addressed to Timothy and the one to Titus—are known as the Pastoral Epistles because, unlike Paul's other letters which are to groups of Christians, these are addressed to individual church leaders. But, it seems that 2 Corinthians may be the most supreme "pastoral epistle" of the New Testament, perhaps of all time.

It is hard enough to be a pastor when you're there with the congregation day after day, and can look them in the eye, sense their mood, discuss their problems with them as they arise, and above all worship and pray with them daily and weekly and all around the year. How much more difficult is it when you're doing your pastoral work, of necessity, at one remove, and through letters, knowing that there are people in the community who are working systematically to undermine you.

This letter has the sure touch of someone who prays for his people, loves them unreservedly, and remains personally open to them, involved with them and vulnerable before them. It is a deeply risky position to be in, and yet Paul persists.

OPEN

Think back over your day today. In what ways do you feel that your words, activities and thoughts have reflected the character of Jesus, and in what ways have they not?

STUDY

1. *Read 2 Corinthians 12:19–13:13.* What anxieties is Paul expressing in verses 12:19–13:4?

2. How do the sins cataloged in 12:20-21 threaten the very life of a Christian community?

3. What does Paul plan to do about the presence of such sins?

4. In 13:4 Paul says that Jesus showed both weakness and power, and that Paul himself does as well. How throughout 2 Corinthians has Paul shown a mixture of weakness and vulnerability on the one hand, and power and strength on the other?

5. What are the consequences of ministering either solely in power or solely in weakness?

6. Why is it so difficult for leaders in ministry to maintain a balance between power and weakness?

7. The Corinthians had been asking Paul for proof that the Messiah really was living and speaking in and through him (13:3). Paul has assured them that plenty of proof will be forthcoming if they are so bold as to challenge him in person. But now he turns the tables on them and suggests that they, too, should submit to a test. What kind of a test is Paul talking about in verses 13:5-10?

8. For Paul, the very center of what it means to be a Christian is that the signs of the Messiah's life, his crucified and risen life, are present in believers. When you look at yourself, how do you see that Jesus is living and active in you?

9. Paul's prayer is that the Corinthians are complete and mature (13:9). What would maturity look like for the Corinthian church?

10. The apparently simple instructions of 13:11-12 are very demanding. Why are they important for a Christian community that has experienced tensions and conflict?

11. The final sentence of 2 Corinthians (13:14) is one of the most famous lines anywhere in Paul—so famous, in fact, that many people who hear it, or say it regularly, don't even realize it is by Paul, and wouldn't be able to find it if they thought it was. It has become a regular prayer, or blessing, in many churches and Christian groups.

How have you seen each aspect of verse 14 in this letter to the Corinthians?

12. How does this verse sum up what being a Christian is all about?

PRAY

Pray specifically for the power of the gospel to be lived out in your life: that, through your weaknesses, the world would see the living King Jesus. Also, spend a few moments praying verse 13 as a blessing for yourself and others.

GUIDELINES FOR LEADERS

My grace is sufficient for you.
(2 Corinthians 12:9)

If leading a small group is something new for you, don't worry. These sessions are designed to flow naturally and be led easily. You may even find that the studies seem to lead themselves!

This study guide is flexible. You can use it with a variety of groups—students, professionals, coworkers, friends, neighborhood or church groups. Each study takes forty-five to sixty minutes in a group setting.

You don't need to be an expert on the Bible or a trained teacher to lead a small group. These guides are designed to facilitate a group's discussion, not a leader's presentation. Guiding group members to discover together what the Bible has to say and to listen together for God's guidance will help them remember much more than a lecture would.

There are some important facts to know about group dynamics and encouraging discussion. The suggestions listed below should equip you to effectively and enjoyably fulfill your role as leader.

PREPARING FOR THE STUDY

1. Ask God to help you understand and apply the passage in your own life. Unless this happens, you will not be prepared to lead others. Pray too for the various members of the group. Ask God to open

your hearts to the message of his Word and motivate you to action.

2. Read the introduction to the entire guide to get an overview of the topics that will be explored.

3. As you begin each study, read and reread the assigned Bible passage to familiarize yourself with it. This study guide is based on the For Everyone series on the New Testament (published by SPCK and Westminster John Knox). It will help you and the group if you have on hand a copy of the companion volume from the For Everyone series both for the translation of the passage found there and for further insight into the passage.

4. Carefully work through each question in the study. Spend time in meditation and reflection as you consider how to respond.

5. Write your thoughts and responses in the space provided in the study guide. This will help you to express your understanding of the passage clearly.

6. It may help to have a Bible dictionary handy. Use it to look up any unfamiliar words, names or places. The glossary at the end of each New Testament for Everyone commentary may likewise be helpful for keeping discussion moving.

7. Reflect seriously on how you need to apply the Scripture to your life. Remember that the group members will follow your lead in responding to the studies. They will not go any deeper than you do.

LEADING THE STUDY

1. At the beginning of your first time together, explain that these studies are meant to be discussions, not lectures. Encourage the members of the group to participate. However, do not put pressure on those who may be hesitant to speak—especially during the first few sessions.

2. Be sure that everyone in your group has a study guide. Encourage the group to prepare beforehand for each discussion by reading the

introduction to the guide and by working through the questions in
each study.

3. Begin each study on time. Open with prayer, asking God to help the
    group to understand and apply the passage.

4. Have a group member read aloud the introduction at the beginning
    of the discussion.

5. Discuss the "Open" question before the Bible passage is read. The
    "Open" question introduces the theme of the study and helps group
    members to begin to open up, and can reveal where our thoughts
    and feelings need to be transformed by Scripture. Reading the pas-
    sage first will tend to color the honest reactions people would other-
    wise give—because they are, of course, supposed to think the way
    the Bible does. Encourage as many members as possible to respond
    to the "Open" question, and be ready to get the discussion going
    with your own response.

6. Have a group member read aloud the passage to be studied as indi-
    cated in the guide.

7. The study questions are designed to be read aloud just as they are writ-
    ten. You may, however, prefer to express them in your own words.

    There may be times when it is appropriate to deviate from the
    study guide. For example, a question may have already been an-
    swered. If so, move on to the next question. Or someone may raise
    an important question not covered in the guide. Take time to dis-
    cuss it, but try to keep the group from going off on tangents.

8. Avoid answering your own questions. An eager group quickly be-
    comes passive and silent if members think the leader will do most
    of the talking. If necessary repeat or rephrase the question until it is
    clearly understood, or refer to the commentary woven into the guide
    to clarify the context or meaning.

9. Don't be afraid of silence in response to the discussion questions.
    People may need time to think about the question before formulat-
    ing their answers.

10. Don't be content with just one answer. Ask, "What do the rest of you think?" or "Anything else?" until several people have given answers to the question.

11. Try to be affirming whenever possible. Affirm participation. Never reject an answer; if it is clearly off-base, ask, "Which verse led you to that conclusion?" or again, "What do the rest of you think?"

12. Don't expect every answer to be addressed to you, even though this will probably happen at first. As group members become more at ease, they will begin to truly interact with each other. This is one sign of healthy discussion.

13. Don't be afraid of controversy. It can be very stimulating. If you don't resolve an issue completely, don't be frustrated. Explain that the group will move on and God may enlighten all of you in later sessions.

14. Periodically summarize what the group has said about the passage. This helps to draw together the various ideas mentioned and gives continuity to the study. But don't preach.

15. Conclude your time together with the prayer suggestion at the end of the study, adapting it to your group's particular needs as appropriate. Ask for God's help in following through on the applications you've identified.

16. End on time.

Many more suggestions and helps for studying a passage or guiding discussion can be found in *How to Lead a LifeGuide Bible Study* and *The Big Book on Small Groups* (both from InterVarsity Press/USA).

Other InterVarsity Press Resources from N. T. Wright

The Challenge of Jesus
N. T. Wright offers clarity and a full accounting of the facts of the life and teachings of Jesus, revealing how the Son of God was also solidly planted in first-century Palestine. *978-0-8308-2200-3, 202 pages, hardcover*

Resurrection
This 50-minute DVD confronts the most startling claim of Christianity—that Jesus rose from the dead. Shot on location in Israel, Greece and England, N. T. Wright presents the political, historical and theological issues of Jesus' day and today regarding this claim. Wright brings clarity and insight to one of the most profound mysteries in human history. Study guide included. *978-0-8308-3435-8, DVD*

Evil and the Justice of God
N. T. Wright explores all aspects of evil and how it presents itself in society today. Fully grounded in the story of the Old and New Testaments, this presentation is provocative and hopeful; a fascinating analysis of and response to the fundamental question of evil and justice that faces believers. *978-0-8308-3398-6, 176 pages, hardcover*

Evil
Filmed in Israel, South Africa and England, this 50-minute DVD confronts some of the major "evil" issues of our time—from tsunamis to AIDS—and puts them under the biblical spotlight. N. T. Wright says there is a solution to the problem of evil, if only we have the honesty and courage to name it and understand it for what it is. Study guide included. *978-0-8308-3434-1, DVD*

Small Faith—Great God
N. T. Wright reminds us that what matters is not how much faith we have as Who our faith is in. Wright looks at the character of the faith God calls us to. He unfolds how dependence, humility and mystery all have a role to play. But the author doesn't ignore the messiness and difficulties of life, when hard times come and the unexpected knocks us down. He opens to us what faith means in times of trial and even in the face of death. Through it all he reminds us, it's not great faith we need: it is faith in a great God. *978-0-8308-3833-2, 176 pages, hardcover*

Justification: God's Plan and Paul's Vision
In this comprehensive account and defense of the crucial doctrine of justification, Wright also responds to critics who have challenged what has come to be called the New Perspective. Ultimately, he provides a chance for those in the

middle of and on both sides of the debate to interact directly with his views and form their own conclusions. *978-0-8308-3863-9, 279 pages, hardcover*

Colossians and Philemon
In Colossians, Paul presents Christ as "the firstborn over all creation," and appeals to his readers to seek a maturity found only Christ. In Philemon, Paul appeals to a fellow believer to receive a runaway slave in love and forgiveness. In this volume N. T. Wright offers comment on both of these important books. *978-0-8308-4242-1, 199 pages, paperback*